Traverse Theatre Company

by Stef Smith

Commissioned by the Traverse Theatre.

First performed at the Traverse Theatre, Edinburgh,
on 2 August 2019.

Company List

Cast
JANE   Louise Ludgate
TONI   Amanda Wright

Creative Team
Writer   Stef Smith
Director   Bryony Shanahan
Set, Costume & Lighting Designer   Kai Fischer
Composer & Sound Designer   Alexandra Faye Braithwaite
Associate Sound Designer   Annie May Fletcher
Assistant Director   Sharon Mackay (supported
                                                   by The Robertson Trust)

Production Team
Production Manager   Kevin McCallum
Chief Electrician   Renny Robertson
Head of Stage   Gary Staerck
Lighting & Sound Technician   Dave Bailey
Lighting & Sound Technician   Joe Davis
Company Stage Manager   Gemma Turner
Deputy Stage Manager   Seána Green
Assistant Stage Manager   Bekah Eva Astles
Costume Supervisor   Victoria Brown
Stage Management Work Placement   Kat Wellman

Company Biographies

Alexandra Faye Braithwaite (Composer & Sound Designer)
Credits include: *How Not To Drown* (ThickSkin/Traverse Theatre Company, co-produced with Tron Theatre and Lawrence Batley Theatre); *Diary of a Madman* (Gate Theatre); *Toast* (PW Productions/The Lowry); *Hamlet, Talking Heads, Rudolf* (Leeds Playhouse); *Cougar, Dealing With Clair, The Rolling Stone* (Orange Tree Theatre); *Romeo and Juliet* (China Plate); *My Name Is Rachel Corrie* (The Faction); *Things of Dry Hours* (Young Vic); *Acceptance* (Hampstead Theatre); *Chicken Soup* (Sheffield Crucible Theatre); *Dublin Carol* (Sherman Theatre); *Room* (Theatre Royal Stratford East/Abbey Theatre); *If I Was Queen* (Almeida Theatre); *The Remains of Maisie Duggan* (Abbey Theatre); *Happy To Help* (Park Theatre); *The Tempest* (Royal & Derngate); *The Future* (The Yard Theatre); *The Audience* and *Juicy and Delicious* (Nuffield Theatre).

Kai Fischer (Set, Costume & Lighting Designer)
Traverse Theatre Company credits include: designs for *Tracks of the Winter Bear* and *Mouthpiece*, and lighting designs for *Gut, How to Disappear, The Pearlfisher* and *I Was a Beautiful Day*.

Further set and lighting design credits include: *Bluebeard's Castle & The 8th Door* (Vanishing Point/Scottish Opera); *The Destroyed Room, The Beautiful Cosmos of Ivor Cutler, Wonderland, Saturday Night* and *Interiors* (Vanishing Point); *Fewer Emergencies* and *Heer Ranjha* (Ankur Productions); *Somersault, Allotment 3* and *4, Mancub, Little Otik* and *Home Caithness* (National Theatre of Scotland); *Grit* (Pachamama); *A Midsummer Night's Dream* and *Wondrous Flitting* (Royal Lyceum Theatre, Edinburgh); *Kind of Silence* (Solar Bear); *Mister Holgado* (Unicorn Theatre) and *One Night Stand* (Nick Underwood).

Lighting design credits include: *The 306: Dusk, Eve, The Tin Forest, Riot of Spring, Pink Mist, Gobbo* and *Julie* (National Theatre of Scotland); *Inés de Castro* (Scottish Opera); *Great Expectations, The Demon Barber, Phedre* and *Cinderella* (Perth Theatre); *Twelfth Night, The Hour We Knew Nothing of Each Other, Cockpit, Charlie Sonata, Irma Vep, Blood and Ice* and *Woyceck* (Royal Lyceum Theatre, Edinburgh); *Tabula Rasa* and *Tomorrow* (Vanishing Point); *Wallace* (The Arches); *Great Expectations* (Beckman Unicorn); *One Million Tiny Plays About Britain, Othello, Museum of Dreams, The Dance of Death* and *Endgame* (Citizens Theatre); *Medea's Children* (Lung Ha Theatre Company); *Brigadoon* and *London Road* (Royal Shakespeare Company); *Oresteia* (SummerScape); *4.48 Psychosis* (Sweetscar); *Macbeth* (Theatre Babe and Hong Kong Cultural Centre) and *The Indian Wants The Bronx* (Young Vic).

Kai's own projects include *Last Dream (On Earth)* (with National Theatre of Scotland and Tron Theatre) and the performance and installation piece *Entartet* (with Vanishing Point and CCA).

Annie May Fletcher (Associate Sound Designer)
Annie trained at London Academy of Music and Dramatic Art (LAMDA).

Sound design credits include: *Highly Sensitive* (Cambridge Junction); *Ad Libido* (Soho Theatre); *The Amber Trap* and *Lobster* (Theatre503); *3 Billion Seconds, Vespertilio, Alcatraz* and *Thomas* (VAULT Festival); *How to Disappear Completely and Never Be Found* and *Humbug! The Hedgehog Who Couldn't Sleep* (Nuffield Southampton Theatres); *Weird* and *Moonfleece* (The Pleasance) and *The Importance of Being Earnest* (Octagon Theatre).

Associate sound designer credits include: *How Not to Drown* (ThickSkin and Traverse Theatre Company, co-produced with Tron Theatre and Lawrence Batley Theatre); *A Hundred Words for Snow* (VAULT Festival/Trafalgar Studios); *Acceptance* (Hampstead Theatre); *Paper. Scissors. Stone* and *Sparks* (VAULT Festival) and *Kanye the First* (HighTide).

Annie is currently Laboratory Associate Sound Designer at Nuffield Southampton Theatres and an Associate Artist with Snapper Theatre Company.

Louise Ludgate (Jane)
Theatre credits: *The Taming of the Shrew* (Sherman Theatre in association with Tron Theatre); *This House* (Headlong Theatre/National Theatre/Chichester Festival Theatre/Jonathan Church Productions); *The Whiphand* (Birmingham Repertory Theatre/Traverse Theatre Company, in association with National Theatre of Scotland); *Lanark: A Life in Three Acts* (Citizens Theatre/Edinburgh International Festival); *Greta* and *Sex and Drugs* (Traverse Theatre Company); *Home, The House of Bernarda Alba, Realism* and *Little Otik* (National Theatre of Scotland); *Mainstream, Casanova* and *Lament* (Suspect Culture); *Iron* (Traverse Theatre Company/Royal Court Theatre); *The Adoption Papers* and *Strawgirl* (Royal Exchange Theatre); *Home Hindrance* (Vanishing Point/Fire Exit); *Sub Rosa* (Citizens Theatre/Fire Exit); *Dig* (Paines Plough); *Jeff Koons* (Actors Touring Company); *Balgay Hill* (Dundee Rep); *13 Sunken Years* (Stellar Quines/Lung Ha Theatre Company in association with the Finnish National Theatre); *Sex & God* (Magnetic North in association with Platform); *Slice* (Oran Mór/Gilded Balloon); *Thank You, Guilty, Resurrection, Out on the Wing, Midge Burgers and The Golden Silence, Moon Walking, Wired, The Date, Days of Wine and Rosie, The Gun, Rumpelstiltskin, Fishwrap, The Course of True Love* and *Losing The Rag* (Oran Mór); *Total Strangers* and *Blackden* (Tron Theatre); *The Crucible, The Devils* and *The Wedding* (The Arches) and *The Hanging Tree* (LookOut Theatre).

Film credits: *City of the Blind* (Fire Exit); *Swung* (Sigma Films); *The Elemental* (Northlight Productions); *Night People* (Newfoundland Film) and *Goodbye Happy Ending* (Fallingwater Films).

Television credits: *River City, Freedom, Spooks, The Key, Sea of Souls* and *Glasgow Kiss* (BBC); *Taggart* and *High Times* (SMG Productions).

Radio credits: *For the Love of Leo, Peoplewatch, Baltamire, Personal Best, Wax Fruit, Best Friends, The Meek, Geordie* and *Lost in Plain Sight* (BBC).

Sharon Mackay (Assistant Director) *Supported by The Robertson Trust*
Sharon graduated with a Bachelor of Arts in Acting from the Royal Conservatoire of Scotland.

Upon graduation she received the Tricia Scott Prize and the Julia Stewart Award for best student of the year. She was a recipient of the Robertson Trust Scholarship 2016–19.

Devising credits: *Debris* (Spoleto Festival Dei 2Mondi, Italy) and *Searching for a Sunny Day* (On the Verge Festival/McLellan Arts Festival).

Bryony Shanahan (Director)
Bryony Shanahan is the incoming joint Artistic Director of the Royal Exchange Theatre, Manchester. She won the Genesis Future Directors award and directed *Trade* at the Young Vic in 2016.

Directing credits include: *Queens of the Coal Age* (Royal Exchange Theatre/New Vic Theatre); *Chicken Soup* (Sheffield Crucible Theatre); *Operation Crucible* (Finborough Theatre/Sheffield Crucible Theatre/59E59 Theaters, New York); *Weald* (Finborough Theatre in association with the Royal Exchange Theatre); *Bitch Boxer* (Soho Theatre/Adelaide Fringe); *Boys Will Be Boys* (National Theatre as part of Women Centre Stage Festival); *You and Me* (Greenwich Theatre) and *Nothing* (Royal Exchange Theatre), winner of the Youth Panel Award at the Manchester Theatre Awards 2017.

Stef Smith (Writer)

Stef Smith is a multi-award-winning writer working for both stage and screen to international acclaim.

Writing credits include: *Girl in the Machine* and *Swallow* (Traverse Theatre Company); *Float* (BBC Scotland); *Nora : A Doll's House* (Citizens Theatre); *The Song Project* and *Human Animals* (Royal Court Theatre); *Acts of Resistance* (Headlong Theatre/Bristol Old Vic); *Love Letters To Europe* (Underbelly); *How to Grow a Nation* (Young Vic); *Remote* (National Theatre Connections Festival); *Tea and Symmetry* (BBC Radio); *Smoke (and Mirrors)* (Traverse Theatre Company and DOT Istanbul for Theatre Uncut); *Back to Back to Back* (Cardboard Citizens); *Cured* (Glasgay! Festival); *Grey Matter* (The Lemon Tree); *Woman of the Year* (Oran Mór) and *Falling/Flying* (Tron Theatre).

Her critically acclaimed show *Roadkill* (Pachamama Productions and Richard Jordan Productions in association with Traverse Theatre Company) won numerous awards, including the Laurence Olivier Award for Outstanding Achievement in an Affiliate Theatre. Stef's Traverse Theatre Company commission *Swallow* won a Scotsman's Fringe First Award and the Scottish Arts Club Theatre Award as part of the Edinburgh Festival Fringe.

Stef has also taken part in the BBC Drama Writers Room and was invited to be part of the Outriders project for Edinburgh International Book festival for which she traveled across Mexico. She is under commission from several theatres and is also an Associate Artist at the Traverse Theatre and Playwrights' Studio Scotland.

Amanda Wright (Toni)

Amanda trained at the Royal Central School of Speech and Drama.

Theatre credits: *Richard II* and *Ralegh: The Treason Trial* (Shakespeare's Globe); *Meek* (Headlong); *Let Me Play The Lion Too* (Barbican/Told By An Idiot); *The Government Inspector* (Birmingham Repertory Theatre); *Dragon* (National Theatre of Scotland); *True* (Deafinitely Theatre); *The 24 Hour Plays* (Old Vic); *Henry V* (Orange Tree Theatre); *Obama-ology* and *AchidiJ's Final Hours* (Finborough Theatre); *Called to Account* (Roundhouse Theatre); *Bloody Sunday* (Tricycle Theatre) and *Big Break* (Hampstead Theatre).

Television credits: *Casualty* and *Doctors* (BBC); *Coronation Street, Midsomer Murders* and *Prime Suspect* (ITV); *Euphoria* (HOT Israel).

About Traverse Theatre Company

As Scotland's new writing theatre, the Traverse Theatre is a dynamic centre for performance, experience and discovery, often referred to as Edinburgh's 'beating heart of the Fringe' in August. Enabling people across society to access and engage with theatre is our fundamental mission.

Our year-round programme bursts with new stories and live performances that challenge, inform and entertain. We empower artists and audiences to make sense of the world today, providing a safe space to question, learn, empathise and – crucially – encounter different people and experiences. Conversation and the coming together of groups are central to a democratic society, and we champion equal expression and understanding.

We commission, produce and programme for existing and future audiences to offer new and exciting experiences for everyone, and our partnerships with other theatre companies and festivals enable us to present a wide range of innovative performances.

The Traverse would not exist without our over-arching passion for talent development and embracing the unexplored. We work with the newest and rawest talent – with an emphasis on the Scottish-based – nurturing it to become the art, artists and performances that can be seen on our stages through a variety of creative learning and literary programmes.

The timely, powerful stories that start life on our stages have global impact, resulting in dozens of tours, productions and translations. We are critically acclaimed and recognised the world over for our originality and artistic risk, which we hope will create some of the most talked-about plays, productions, directors, writers and actors for years to come.

Find out more about the Traverse: **traverse.co.uk**

With thanks

The Traverse Theatre extends grateful thanks to all those who generously support our work, including those who prefer their support to remain anonymous.

Traverse Theatre Supporters
Diamond – Alan and Penny Barr, Katie Bradford, Kirsten Lamb, David Rodgers
Platinum – Angus McLeod, Iain Millar
Gold – Carola Bronte-Stewart
Silver – Bridget M. Stevens, Allan Wilson, Judy & Steve
Bronze – Barbara Cartwright, Alex Oliver & Duncan Stephen

Trusts, Foundations and Grants
Anderson Anderson & Brown Charitable Initiative
Backstage Trust
British Council: UK/India 2017 Fund
British Council Scotland and Creative Scotland: UK in Japan 2019–20
The Cross Trust
Dr David Summers Charitable Trust
The Fidelio Charitable Trust
The Foyle Foundation
The Gannochy Trust
Garrick Charitable Trust
Idlewild Trust
The JMK Trust
The JTH Charitable Trust
John Thaw Foundation
The Leche Trust
The Mackintosh Foundation
The McGlashan Charitable Trust
Murdoch Forrest Charitable Trust
The Nimar Charitable Trust
The Noël Coward Foundation (noelcoward.org)
The Robertson Trust
The Russell Trust
The Steel Charitable Trust
The Great Britain Sasakawa Foundation
The Teale Charitable Trust
The Turtleton Charitable Trust
The W M Mann Foundation

Traverse Theatre Production Supporters
Allander Print
Cotterell & Co
Paterson SA Hairdressing

Special thanks to
National Theatre of Scotland and the King's Theatre, Edinburgh

Grant Funders

Traverse Theatre (Scotland) is a Limited Company (SC076037) and a Scottish Charity (SC002368) with its Registered Office at 10 Cambridge Street, Edinburgh, Scotland, EH1 2ED.

Traverse Theatre

The Company

Laura Antone	Development Assistant
Dave Bailey	Lighting & Sound Technician
Fiona Campbell	Audience Experience Manager
Linda Crooks	Executive Producer & Chief Executive
Megan Davies-Varnier	Deputy Box Office Manager
Joe Davis	Lighting & Sound Technician
Isobel Dew	Assistant Producer – Traverse Theatre Programme
Anna Docherty	Press & Media Officer
David Drummond	General Manager
Danielle Fentiman	Producer
Ellen Gledhill	Development Manager
Mollie Hodkinson	Administration Apprentice
Cecil Lane	Ticketing & Customer Service Officer
Kath Lowe	Front of House Manager
Kevin McCallum	Head of Production
Ruth McEwan	Senior Producer
Lauren McLay	Marketing & Media Assistant
Suzanne Murray	Bar Café Manager
Victoria Murray	Head of Brand & Audience
Gareth Nicholls	Interim Artistic Director
Alice Pelan	Finance & Administration Assistant
Julie Pigott	Head of Finance & Operations
Pauleen Rafferty	Payroll & HR Manager
Sunniva Ramsay	Creative Producer (Learning)
Anna Richardson	Ticketing & Customer Service Officer
Renny Robertson	Chief Electrician
Jonathan Rowett	Bar Café Senior Supervisor
Gary Staerck	Head of Stage
Sabino Tidrick	Senior Chef
Kyriakos Vogiatzis	Marketing & Campaigns Officer
Eleanor White	Literary Assistant

Also working for the Traverse

Dylan Adams, Eleanor Agnew, Charlotte Anderson, Lindsay Anderson, Shellie-Ann Barrowcliffe, Alannah Beaton, Carena Brogan, Sarah Brooks-Reynolds, Victoria Brown, Emma Campbell, Peter Carson, Hannah Cornish Isla Cowan, Fibi Cowley, Stephen Cox, Robin Crane, Rachel Cullen, Koralia Daskalaki, Amy Dawson, Matt Donnelly, Molly Duffield, Callum Finlay, Andrew Gannon, Avril Gardiner, Laura Hawkins, Sunny Howie, Catherine Idle, Adam James, Laura Jenkinson, Nikki Kalkman, Jonathan Kennedy, David Kramaric, Sean Langtree, Laura Laria, John Lynskey, Tanya MacDonald, Ewa Malicka, Rebecca Martin, Alan Massie, Kieran McCruden, Rachael McDougall, Alison McFarlane, Olivia McIntosh, Kirsty McIntyre, Will Moore, Chris Mundy, Breanna Murtagh, Niamh O'Donoghue, Suzanne Peden, Jessi Rich, Clare Ross, Theodora Sakellaridou, Kolbrun Sigfusdottir, Rob Small, David Stabback, Ewan Sullivan, Joanne Sykes, Linda Taylor, Jac Thain, Elena Tirado, Andy Turnbull, Nick Waddell, Rebecca Waites, Jason Wang, Rosie Ward, Sam Watson, Emma Whyte, Jonathan Whyte, Sophie Wright

Associate Artists

Emma Callander
Rob Drummond
Gary McNair
Morna Pearson
Tim Price
Stef Smith

IASH/Traverse Creative Fellow for 2019

Lewis Hetherington

Channel 4 Playwrights' Scheme Writer in Residence

Meghan Tyler

Traverse Theatre Board of Directors

Sir John Elvidge (Chair)
Morag Ballantyne
Myriam Madden
Dave Moutrey
Donna Reynolds
Christopher Wynn

ENOUGH

Stef Smith

For Rose.

*One of the kindest and smartest people on the planet,
who through the years has selflessly offered her support
as I wrote this play. She has taught me a life-changing amount
about both art and friendship.*

I will be forever thankful that we chose each other.

Acknowledgements

My sincere appreciation to the cast, crew and creatives who were involved in the premiere production of *Enough*. And of course, to the brilliant team at the Traverse Theatre.

My thanks to Orla O'Loughlin, who encouraged me to write this play and has been crucial to its evolution. Further thanks to all those who have been part of its development, in particular: Rosie Kellagher, Shauna MacDonald, Ros Sydney and Anita Vettesse.

As ever, thank you to my agent Davina Shah, the team at MLR, the team at Nick Hern Books and my incredibly supportive theatre-making peers.

I'd also like to thank my friends and family for the text messages, cups of coffee, glasses of dry white wine and for always listening. This play makes me think of all the wonderful women I have my life – I am very lucky and you are all so very brilliant.

Finally, thank you to Bryony Shanahan. For her compassion and craft, her friendship and fire.

S.S.

'You have to pick the places you don't walk away from.'

Joan Didion

'I think the wrong things are kept private.'

Nan Goldin

Characters

JANE, *forties*
TONI, *forties*

Both are flight attendants and have been friends for many years.

Note

A forward slash (/) denotes a line running into the next without a pause.

There are very few stage directions; imagine it as you wish.

This text went to press before the end of rehearsals and so may differ slightly from the play as performed.

TONI	When I walk into a room, in my uniform.
JANE	There is a look that gets thrown my way.
TONI	When I walk into a room, in my uniform.
JANE	It's as if for a second everything stops.
TONI	For I am the image of escape.
JANE	A symbol of sex appeal and sightseeing.
TONI	All high heels and higher standards.
JANE	Navy and nylons.
TONI	With nails polished into pearls.
JANE	And it's just this way I /
TONI	It's just this way I /
JANE	And it's just this way /
TONI	When I walk into a room, in my uniform.
JANE	There is a look that gets thrown my way.
TONI	When I walk into a room, in my uniform.
JANE	It's as if for a second everything stops.
TONI	It's just this way I /
JANE	And it's just this way /
TONI	This hotel is a fucking shithole.
	And you know what – fuck you, Jane.
JANE	When I walk into a room, in my uniform.
TONI	You know what, Jane?
	You fucking know what, Jane?
	Fuck you, Jane.

JANE	There is a look that gets thrown my way.
TONI	I am never drinking with you again.
JANE	It's as if for a second everything stops.
TONI	You.
JANE	For I am the image of escape.
TONI	You should know better.
JANE	A symbol of sex appeal and sightseeing.
TONI	I am easily encouraged and you take advantage of that.
JANE	And it's just this way I /
TONI	For fucking years, you've taken advantage of that.
JANE	It's just this way /
TONI	You are a terrible friend. You're a terrible fucking friend.
JANE	Excuse me? What did you just say?
TONI	When I walk into a room, in my uniform.
JANE	Because I wasn't the one pouring those drinks.
TONI	There is a look that gets thrown my way.
JANE	You're a grown woman, Toni.
TONI	It's as if for a second everything stops.
JANE	You.
TONI	For I am the image of escape.
JANE	You're the one who should know better.
TONI	A symbol of sex appeal and sightseeing.
JANE	I can't help the fact that I am fun to be around.
TONI	And it's just this way I /
JANE	I can't help the fact that together we have fun.

TONI   It's just this way /

JANE   Isn't that a good thing? To have fun?

TONI   I was sick this morning. That wasn't fun.

JANE   You didn't seem that drunk.

TONI   I'm quitting drinking.

JANE   You'd quit breathing first.

TONI   Well... maybe I'll just drink a little less.

JANE   Let me know how that works out for you.

TONI   You've such little faith in me.

JANE   No, I'm just realistic. And by the way you've got lipstick on your teeth... but that colour suits you. Makes your eyes all – wow.

TONI   And it's glamour and grace.

JANE   And it's manners and managing.

TONI   And it's turbulence and turbos and tickets.

JANE   And it's just passing through and just moving on.

TONI   And it's thirty thousand feet of freedom.

JANE   And it's just coming and going and /

TONI   It's just /

JANE   Take-offs /

TONI   And landings.

JANE   Doing anything nice with your days off?

TONI   I don't know.

JANE   Will you see that... boy.

TONI   Man. He is very much a man.

JANE   Did you just blush?

TONI   No.

JANE	Doesn't he live in the middle of nowhere? Doesn't it take you hours to get there?
TONI	I like that it takes hours. On my days off all I've got is hours.
JANE	I like my husband in reaching distance.
TONI	Except when you don't.
JANE	Well, you can't like everyone all of the time.
TONI	What does that mean?
JANE	Nothing. It means nothing.
TONI	Is that right?
JANE	And I am an authority of the air who takes care of your lunch and your life.
TONI	Just in case. Just in case anything should go wrong.
JANE	And in the air, there is very rarely such a thing as a little wrong.
TONI	Because either everything is fine, or death is just seconds away.
JANE	Because when everything is going wrong /
TONI	When everything is going to shit /
JANE	And the world turns upside down /
TONI	Or the oxygen runs out /
JANE	Or turbulence makes your body float above itself /
TONI	Or the fear has been too much for too long and you can't catch your breath and you think this might kill you, you genuinely think this feeling in you might kill you, because the fear has been too much for too long and you can't catch your breath and you think this might kill you, you genuinely think this feeling in you might kill you. Because the fear has been too much for too long, too much for too long, too much for too long, too much for too long, too much for too long /

JANE   You turn and look at the cabin crew. In a moment of emergency /

TONI   Just turn and look at the cabin crew.

JANE   Three minutes. It takes three minutes for an aeroplane to fall from thirty-three thousand feet to the ground. And I've given a lot of thought to those three minutes, one hundred and eighty seconds. I feel at peace with those seconds and minutes and hours and days and years. I'd think about my children and my husband and I'd just fall.

TONI   And I'd just fall.

JANE   One hundred and eighty

TONI   One hundred and seventy-nine

JANE   One hundred and seventy-eight

TONI   One hundred and seventy-seven

JANE   One hundred and seventy-six

TONI   One hundred and seventy-/

JANE   Five days off. A whole five days off. You're lucky.

TONI   Would you mind feeding my cat? I can't ask my cat-sitter to do more hours, I already feel judged by her.

JANE   Where are you going?

TONI   Away.

JANE   Isn't it a holiday to be at home?

TONI   No.

JANE   Your cat hates me.

TONI   He hates everything – that's why I love him. Takes a lot of commitment to hate everything that much.

JANE   Sounds like my mother.

TONI   How is she?

JANE   Old. Are you away all week?

TONI   No. I'm flying to Hong Kong on Tuesday. You?

JANE   Milan then St Petersburg.

TONI   And Delhi

JANE   And Detroit

TONI   And Moscow

JANE   And Melbourne

TONI   And Mexico City

JANE   And home.

The best thing about home is coming back to it. Those thirty seconds of the relief of returning. It washes over me like a wave. I hold it close, hold it tight, as if it could slip away at any second, as if I could slip away. As if I could fall through the seconds, between my breaths and my heartbeats, I could fall through the seconds, the minutes, the hours, if I wasn't careful. And I'm so careful.

TONI   And I am /

JANE   I am /

TONI   I am safety /

JANE   I am sex /

TONI   You can hear the wheels of my suitcase in the corridors of airports and hotels.

JANE   Each designed to make life feel compact and complete.

TONI   Ageless expanses that are both comfortable and wipeable.

JANE   And the air is a mixture of frenzy and fatigue.

TONI   It's just passing through and it's just moving on.

JANE   It's all shiny and slippery and unspecific.

TONI   And a man rubs his hand over her skirt.

JANE   And a man talks over her as she tries to ask
            a question.

TONI   And I glide through it all /

JANE   With glamour and grace.

TONI   I am safety.

JANE   I glide through it all.

TONI   I am sex.

JANE   With glamour and grace.

TONI   I am here to serve you.

JANE   And I am here to serve you.

TONI   I am here.

JANE   I am here.

TONI   I am here.

JANE   I am /

TONI   Have you seen the news recently?

JANE   Yeah, terrible.

TONI   Isn't it awful?

JANE   Just awful.

TONI   What do we /

JANE   I don't know.

TONI   And just like that. A tiny tremor happens below
            her. Almost unnoticeable.

JANE   The ground almost imperceptibly groans.

TONI   Something is beginning to /

JANE   Something is /

TONI   What?

JANE   Didn't say anything.

TONI   I arrive at his door.

JANE   Home.

TONI   And there is a split second, before I ring the doorbell, where a switch in me – flicks. Like passing your hand through a flame, there is part of you that wants to be burned.

JANE   Home.

TONI   I arrive into his arms.

JANE   The relief of returning.

TONI   And I run my hands through his hair.

JANE   And I am greeted by two faces who have my eyes and their father's tangle of tender toughness.

TONI   I drop to my knees.

JANE   I drop my suitcase and my keys.

TONI   I hold on to his legs to keep myself steady.

JANE   They drop their pieces of plastic, their toys and teddies.

TONI   (*Together.*) And he stands in front of me.

JANE   (*Together.*) And they stand in front of me.

JANE   Mum.

TONI   And his zip is in between my lips.

JANE   Only two people in a world of billions call me Mum.

TONI   And his touch.

JANE   And that still surprises me.

TONI   And his touch.

JANE   And they hug me as if I have been gone for a century.

TONI   And his hands begin to move down me. His palms, all passion and purpose.

JANE   And it feels like in three days they've grown three inches. And I tell myself not to worry.

TONI   Hurry.

JANE   Don't worry.

TONI   Hurry.

JANE   Don't worry.

TONI   And I am greedy for his touch.

JANE   Their smiles shine.

TONI   Gorging myself on his skin.

JANE   As sure as sun through thin glass.

TONI   Grasping. Gasping.

JANE   And they are more than I could have ever asked.

TONI   Breathing. Beating.

JANE   And I press their bodies into mine.

TONI   Craving. Clinging.

JANE   And I can feel their heartbeats as I kiss their soft faces.

TONI   And in between my body and his, I close the spaces.

JANE   (*Together.*) I want you close.

TONI   (*Together.*) I want you close.

JANE   I'm here now.

TONI   I'm ready now.

JANE   I'm here now.

TONI   I'm ready now.

JANE   I'm here now.

TONI	I'm ready now.
JANE	I'm here now.
TONI	I'm ready now.
JANE	And she falls through the minutes.
TONI	She falls through the windows of their words.
JANE	She soaks in his skin.
TONI	She watches them, as if she sits a million miles away. Her husband, her children, smiling, laughing, sharing the moment and she takes herself to the toilet and locks the door.
JANE	And she lies next to him. Too tired to sleep. And her hips hurt from where he held her. Sometimes, his grip is so tight, for a split second it scares her.
TONI	She sits in the solitude, the silence and stillness. While an unspecific and soft sadness slowly sets in. She pulls herself back from herself by watching the way the light falls on the wall.
JANE	And sometimes she craves his touch so much, for a split second it scares her. And she can feel her blood beat around her body at the thought of his touch. Her breath is almost pulled out from her.
TONI	And on the wall she can see faint lines of colour creeping through the paint. Something is beginning to show itself. That won't do, she thinks. That won't do at all. And she promises to make it perfect. And she likes the feel of purpose to that promise.
JANE	And she places her hand on her heart. Trying to slow it. Telling her heart to slow down.
TONI	And she tells herself she has everything she wants.
JANE	I have everything I want.
TONI	Slow. Down.
	Phone call.

JANE   Sweetheart. It's me.

            I'm not sure if you're picking up phone calls or
            just... well... I'm here with your feline. Actually,
            he is hiding somewhere. But I swear I saw him
            a split second ago... oh, he took a massive shit on
            your bed, so I've washed your sheets.

            Anyway, I saw you had a bottle of Merlot on the
            counter so I'm going to sit and drink it. Hope
            that's okay. I'll replace it.

TONI   And it's midnight and there is little left of the
            Merlot.

JANE   John is with the kids and I need...

TONI   Her phone blinks blue with messages and missed
            calls.

JANE   I just need...

TONI   Voicemails with her children in the background
            and a husband with the sound of anticipation and
            affection on his lips.

JANE   I just thought I'd live your life for an evening.

TONI   She sits in the softness of the sofa, in the seclusion
            of someone else's home.

JANE   I miss you.

TONI   She runs her thumb along her tummy.

JANE   Call me.

TONI   On her stomach is a scar that brought a child into the
            world. A scar that she didn't want but had no choice.
            A scar that saved her life and then her child's.

            Her hand moves to her thighs. The raised ridges of
            sorrow and anger and the unexpressed and the
            unexplained. Self-inflicted symbols from an
            earlier self. More than most she knows the line
            between power and pain is the size of a scar.

And for a moment she feels terrified for her children. Her children who will one day be teenagers. Life has become so complicated and so small. Like a Swiss Army knife.

Shiny. Serrated. Small.

And responsibility wraps itself around her and on nights like tonight she can't tell if that is the feeling of a necklace or a noose.

Silence.

JANE   Do you want another drink?

TONI   You're drinking quickly.

JANE   I don't know why people love this city.

TONI   Well, I love this city.

JANE   You love every city.

TONI   But I particularly love this city.

JANE   It's just a city, the same as any other city.

TONI   Well, if that doesn't sound like cabin crew.

JANE   Hundreds of cities, hundreds of airports and they are all the same.

TONI   That's not true.

JANE   The scenery may change but the situation doesn't. Buildings and bridges and buses and people and pigeons and pollution and dirt and /

TONI   Are you going for the promotion?

JANE   What? Team leader?

TONI   It's more money.

JANE   It's more bullshit. You're tempted?

TONI   Don't you think I'm too elegant for economy.

JANE   Elegance is overrated. But go for it. They'd be lucky to have you.

TONI	Maybe.
JANE	What day is it today?
TONI	I've no idea.
JANE	And it's Darwin.
TONI	And Indianapolis.
JANE	And Istanbul.
TONI	And Rome.
JANE	And Recife.
TONI	And Warsaw.
JANE	And I work to make my house flawless.
TONI	And I keep pushing for that promotion.
JANE	It's ploughing every penny and piece of me into making it picture perfect.
TONI	And I'm working every hour I can to prove I am good, great, perfect. Scraping the skin off me, as proof.
JANE	Ploughing every piece of me.
TONI	Scratching my skin off.
JANE	And something somewhere begins to shift.
TONI	Rocks and rubble rub up against me.
JANE	The ground begins to grind against itself.
TONI	The dirt begins to groan.
JANE	It's just soil and soot and shit and stuff, that crushes up against /
TONI	Show me where it hurts.
JANE	Show me how it hurts.
TONI	Show me /
JANE	Have you seen the news?

TONI   It's just awful.

JANE   And all of history just /

TONI   All of history just /

JANE   And we distract ourselves.

TONI   And we distract ourselves with dazzling things.

JANE   And stare at skylines that shine in the sun.

TONI   Escape into the twinkle of twilight.

JANE   We allow life to become small.

TONI   You never did replace that wine.

JANE   What?

TONI   You drank my Merlot.

JANE   I cleaned up your cat's shit.

TONI   Point taken.

JANE   I think we bonded. Me and the cat.

TONI   Careful, you'll get the kids that kitten they want.

JANE   I said I won't get a kitten until we get a new kitchen.

TONI   Fuck.

JANE   What?

TONI   That is the most boring sentence I have ever heard.

JANE   My kitchen isn't boring.

TONI   It's quite boring.

JANE   You think my life is boring.

TONI   Weren't you in Tokyo last week?

JANE   I was in a hotel room in Tokyo last week.

TONI   You could have gone out.

JANE	You try having two children with chest infections. I haven't slept in a week. It's amazing I am upright.
TONI	Your children are always ill.
JANE	How long till take-off?
TONI	Fifteen minutes.
JANE	How is your guy?
TONI	Fine.
JANE	Is it something serious?
TONI	No.
JANE	Just sex?
TONI	Just sex.
JANE	I suppose it's nice to have hobbies.
TONI	Do you and John still have sex?
JANE	Why do you think the kids go to gymnastics on a Friday night?
TONI	The smallness of life slips in.
JANE	I'd actually been thinking about…
TONI	The normality of nothingness.
JANE	Trying to get some time away. Just me.
TONI	Because all of history is /
JANE	I think I need some time away.
TONI	Show me where it hurts.
JANE	Show me how it hurts.
TONI	Because the beauty of something is that it is nearly always nothing.
JANE	Continents collide /
TONI	A Swiss Army knife of a life.
JANE	Because there is so much life to live.

TONI	Have you seen the news recently?
JANE	Yeah, terrible.
TONI	It's awful.
JANE	There is too much life to live.
TONI	And a man whistles at her from over the road.
JANE	And a man bumps into her and knocks her to her knees without an apology.
TONI	I am safety.
JANE	I am sex /
TONI	I glide through it with /
JANE	I stand in an aisle of tins and change, attempting to find the right shade of something. Clutching paint samples as if they were sacred.
TONI	And I'm two hours late because of work and so, when I arrive at his place, his face is petrol and I'm the match.
JANE	DIY dads flutter around me.
TONI	And I attempt to kiss and make up.
JANE	Standing in front of a thousand shades of blue.
TONI	And he slips his fists around my wrists.
JANE	When did we begin to need so many choices?
TONI	He holds my arms above my head and kisses me, hard.
JANE	And every time I choose a colour it's wrong. The room is inches smaller from all the layers of paint.
TONI	And he begins to bite my skin.
JANE	Though, this time I am certain I've got it perfect.
TONI	And I try to wriggle away but his grip tightens.

JANE   And this will be the year, we'll finish the house
            and it will be perfect. Complete.

TONI   Suddenly he seems huge and I push him away.

JANE   It will be absolutely perfect.

TONI   And then his fist is coming towards my face and
            I am surprised by the sound of his skin slapping
            mine.

JANE   Absolutely perfect.

TONI   And the next thing I know I'm on my knees.
            And he wraps his arms around me, whispering
            his apologies.

            And all of his words just rush past, fast because all
            I can feel is fire across my face.

            He hit me.

            He fucking hit me.

JANE   And as she gets up, she pushes him down and
            punches him in the chest and she punches him,
            and she punches him, and she punches him. Her
            face flushes, and her fists ache as he backs off with
            an apology. And she feels the ground begin to
            shake. The low rumble of something deep and
            dark trying to get out.

TONI   The ground begins to groan.

JANE   Have you watched the news?

TONI   The ground trembles.

JANE   Have you seen what's happening?

TONI   Something is working its way to the surface.

JANE   And she waits in her car, parked outside his house.
            Eating a sweet she found in the glove
            compartment and she sits quietly, and she chews
            and chews and chews /

TONI   And I drive for hours and hours in silence. Until
            there is no petrol in the tank and no tears left to
            cry. And I sit, looking at the stars and I feel like
            less than a speck. And my skin burns with the
            embers of someone else's anger. And I push this
            down and I push this away and all I have is the
            pushing down and all I have is the pushing away
            and all I have is the pushing down and all I have is
            the pushing away and all I have is the pushing
            down and all I have is the…

JANE   And the ground below her growls.

TONI   Before we take off, your captain asks that you
            familiarise yourself with our safety procedures
            and equipment.

JANE   Whenever the sign is on, fasten your seatbelt
            securely. Insert the metal tag into the buckle and
            tighten by pulling on the loose end.

TONI   To undo the belt, simply lift up the metal flap on
            the buckle and pull apart.

JANE   Lift up the metal flap on the buckle and pull apart.

TONI   And pull apart.

JANE   And pull apart.

TONI   And pull apart.

JANE   How was your time off?

TONI   Oh. Fine. Thanks.

JANE   No details?

TONI   Nothing exciting happened.

JANE   That's unlike you.

TONI   My life is not as exciting as you think it is.

JANE   Were you seeing that guy?

TONI   Why?

JANE   Just wondering.

TONI   I've gone off him.

JANE   Why?

TONI   I just… I didn't think he was right for me.

JANE   You're too quick to dismiss people. You should give him a second chance.

TONI   I should do a lot of things.

JANE   Be careful of regrets.

TONI   Like you don't have a couple.

JANE   I work really hard at not regretting.

TONI   You've painted your bathroom a thousand different shades of blue. Tell me you don't regret that.

JANE   I'll get it right eventually.

TONI   I'm sure you will.

JANE   You think my life is ridiculous, don't you?

TONI   No.

JANE   Well, maybe my life is ridiculous. But I think I've earnt it. The ridiculousness of it.

TONI   I didn't say your life was ridiculous.

JANE   You didn't have to.

TONI   Are you okay?

JANE   I'm fine. Now, please can we get another drink?

TONI   Show me where it hurts.

JANE   And it's just this way I /

TONI   Show me how it hurts.

JANE   It's just this /

TONI   All of history just /

JANE   And we drink until it's closer to dawn than dusk. And we smoke secret cigarettes and we laugh, and we lie. Lies like splinters. So small you only notice them when it hurts for them to trip off your lips. And we drink. And we drink. And we /

TONI   I lay in bed. Sweating out Sauvignon Blanc and trying to get the room to stop spinning. I grip on to the bedsheets and swear I'll never drink again if only this would end.

And from below I begin to hear this groan.

This guttural groan.

And the ground begins to shake. The noise of something cracking and splitting and breaking away.

The distant noise of tremors and change and growing and grasping and groaning.

Something trying to get out.

Something trying to find me.

Something I can't hold on to, something I can't get let go. Something I can't hold on to, something I can't get let go. Something I can't hold on to, something I can't get let go.

JANE   And Miami and Madrid.

TONI   Something I can't hold /

JANE   Helsinki and Hong Kong.

TONI   Something I can't /

JANE   Zurich and Zagreb.

TONI   Something I /

JANE   Tokyo and Tijuana.

TONI   Something /

JANE   And she wakes up. And she has bitten through her
            own lip.

            Blood on her pillow. Sweat on her sheets.

            It takes her nearly two minutes to realise it was
            just a dream. Well, a nightmare.

TONI   Just a nightmare.

JANE   And her face burns with the tear gas of tears.

            She opens the door to her hotel room and sees
            nothing but a badly lit corridor. A neon light winks
            and a child cries down the hall. She double-locks
            the door, to keep the outside out and the inside in.

            She turns on the distraction of the television.
            The news is the only noise in a language she
            understands. Another bomb has gone off
            somewhere north of nowhere.

TONI   Sweetheart. It's me.

JANE   She picks out dirt from under her nails.

TONI   I'm just calling to say… hello. So, hello.

JANE   She picks out dirt from under her nails.

TONI   I suppose I'm feeling a bit… it's just… Can you
            call me?

JANE   And she runs a bath and for the next three hours
            she scrubs her nails so hard they bleed. Then she
            sits in cold water and cries. Because in this hotel
            north-west of nowhere in particular she can't think
            of anything else to do.

TONI   And even though her friend is calling her, she lets
            it go to voicemail. Enjoying the silence of her
            children sleeping and her husband on a rare night
            out without her.

            She goes into her bedroom and pinpoints a
            particular drawer in a room filled with drawers

filled with stuff that she doesn't look at from one year to the next. But there is a weight to it to this drawer. She pulls it and it's the noise of metal moving on itself – coins. It's filled with foreign coins.

Brass and silver and gold. Ones, tens, hundreds. Ten thousand somethings from that time she went somewhere. Coins from countries that no longer exist.

One by one she holds them. She counts them. She rubs her thumb over them. Her hands begin to hold their metallic scent, like blood. She focuses every inch of her security on these small metal symbols. A reminder that the world is big.

A reminder that she is very small. And it takes off the weight of expectation to know that she is nothing but a notch in time.

JANE	And below her the ground shakes.
TONI	And in the distance there is grasping and groans.
JANE	Something is trying to get out.
TONI	Have you watched the news?
JANE	Something is rising up.
TONI	Have you seen what's happening?
JANE	Something is coming back.
TONI	You know I was thinking it's been years since we've been in this city together.
JANE	I like it. The way the light is just…
TONI	That's not like you.
JANE	What?
TONI	It's been a long time since you've said you actually liked a place that isn't your own home.

JANE	I used to love travelling.
TONI	What's changed?
JANE	What hasn't changed.
TONI	Your terrible taste in music.
JANE	I like that country music tells a story – I can't help it.

And it's just nice to go back, isn't it? Go back to where you've been. Sometimes. It just reminds you of / |
TONI	What?
JANE	Yourself.
TONI	When I walk into a room, in my /
JANE	There is a look that gets /
TONI	When I walk into a room, in my /
JANE	It's as if for a second /
TONI	For I am the image of /
JANE	A symbol of /
TONI	All high heels and higher /
JANE	Navy and nylons /
TONI	With nails polished into /
JANE	And it's just this way I /
TONI	It's just this way I /
JANE	And it's just this way /
TONI	I've not been sleeping great. All these crazy dreams. Thinking about going to a doctor to get something to knock me out. I just need a night or two. You know? The difference a good night's sleep makes.
JANE	When did you last sleep?

TONI   I'm sleeping… it's the dreaming I can't stand.

JANE   You should have called me.

TONI   I did. I left a voicemail.

JANE   You should have called again.

TONI   I shouldn't need to.

JANE   Don't be angry – I was looking after the kids by myself. You should have called again.

TONI   Maybe.

JANE   What is that supposed to mean?

TONI   It means… maybe.

JANE   And she reaches into her handbag for her lipstick and as she moves her fingers into it, she suddenly feels them touch – sand. Inches of sand in her handbag. Soft and cold like it's been sitting there for centuries. And she fumbles to find her lipstick in it and she doesn't flinch, she doesn't let anyone know.

TONI   Sand.

JANE   Soil.

TONI   Soot.

JANE   Grit.

TONI   Dirt.

JANE   And she doesn't let anyone know.

TONI   As she reaches for her glass, she turns it so to see her own reflection and she doesn't see anything. And the ground below her groans. She slides herself, so she might also see herself in the reflection of the glass table and she can't see anything, and the table begins to tremble.

JANE   I am /

TONI   I am /

JANE	You alright?
TONI	Yeah fine.
JANE	I work to make my house flawless.
TONI	I keep pushing for that promotion.
JANE	It's ploughing every penny and piece of /
TONI	Working every hour to prove I am /
JANE	Ploughing every piece of /
TONI	I will /
JANE	I can't /
TONI	I'm not /
JANE	I won't /
TONI	And as the ground trembles the women don't even look at each other.
JANE	Both feel it but neither mentions it.
TONI	They just sit silently and sip their Chardonnay.
JANE	They pick at their painted nails.
TONI	There is no end /
JANE	There is no defining moment /
TONI	And they stare at skylines that shine in the sun.
JANE	Escape into the twinkle of twilight.
TONI	Want to get drunk?
JANE	More than anything.
TONI	I take her hand in mine and our eyes connect and without talking she has told me a thousand things.
JANE	I order another bottle and before we know it it's disappeared. On nights like these – alcohol seems to evaporate.

TONI   And she pours another and another and another
         and that shift from sadness into giddiness starts
         from the soles of my feet and works up.

JANE   A smile falls on her face. A smile with a shade of
         sadness, a shade of silliness and more than a touch
         of wanting to fuck things up.

TONI   And the laughter in the air is thick and dirty and
         deep.

JANE   As if all of life is a joke and we've finally just
         understood the punchline and it's us.

TONI   And wine turns into whisky and there is a fire in
         the air tonight, a fierceness in the air tonight. We
         forget ourselves.

JANE   And in the bathroom she passes me a powder and
         we pull it into ourselves. I have thirty seconds of
         thinking about my children and it takes a few
         breaths, it takes a few heartbeats but suddenly,
         I feel certain that everything will be okay.

TONI   And it takes a few breaths. It takes a few
         heartbeats. And that hollow inside of me heals.
         The wholeness that comes with the high.

JANE   Driven to dance and drink and pour ourselves into
         a room full of light and sound and bodies banging
         into each other.

TONI   And we are surrounded by sound and light, on a
         night where I am pretty sure we are indestructible.

JANE   And I take her by the hands.

TONI   And her palms pulse in mine. And I pull her close.

JANE   The softness.

TONI   The tenderness.

JANE   I wrap my body into hers.

TONI	And our lips touch.
	(*Together.*) I love you. I really love you.
JANE	(*Together.*) I love you. I really love you.
TONI	And the dirt /
JANE	And the sand /
TONI	And the shit /
JANE	And the stuff /
TONI	And there is a shudder /
JANE	And a shake /
TONI	And a shiver /
JANE	Between them /
TONI	And beneath them /
JANE	They fall through their breaths /
TONI	Between their heartbeats /
JANE	Through the seconds and the minutes and the hours.
TONI	They are nothing but nerve endings. Animals and atoms /
JANE	The ground below them shakes and they cling on to each other.
TONI	The sound of breathing and groaning and /
JANE	Shouts and screams and /
TONI	Voices that sound like engines /
JANE	Voices that sound like foxes fucking /
TONI	And the ground just /
JANE	It feels like it might /
TONI	And she is sex.
JANE	She is desire.

TONI   She is an escape.

JANE   And I am here.

TONI   I am here.

JANE   I am here.

TONI   I am here.

JANE   I am here.

TONI   I am here.

JANE   I am here.

TONI   I am here.

JANE   And after saying goodnight for what felt like
            a lifetime, I pour myself in a cab.

TONI   And there is a burning in my belly that suggests
            that I am not done yet.

JANE   And the world begins to spin and suddenly I feel
            incredibly thin.

TONI   As I walk the street with the feeling of fire in my
            feet. And I can't stop picking at the dirt beneath
            my nails.

JANE   And all the blood rushes to my face.

TONI   A woman comes up to me and she asks if I want
            a little fun.

JANE   And my stomach crumbles into itself.

TONI   And she tells me what she is willing to do and for
            how much.

JANE   And I can't keep it in.

TONI   And a flicker of someone I don't know strikes
            through me like a match. And I nod and tell her
            what I want and hand her a fistful of notes.

JANE   I shout at the taxi driver to stop and open the door
            to be sick on the street.

TONI	And she takes me to a patch of grass and darkness and takes off her top and places my hands on her breasts.
JANE	And I pour out of the door, scraping my knees on the ground as I go and the taxi drives off with curse words being hurled at me.
TONI	And I grip on to her skin. And it's nails and lips and tongues and fingers and fucking.
JANE	Blood trickles from my knees as I sit and attempt to focus on the stars.
TONI	As I push her face into my lap, I stare at those stars. She puts her lips around my zip.
JANE	(*Together.*) Fuck.
TONI	(*Together.*) Fuck.
	The sky looks beautiful tonight.
JANE	Nothing but a notch in time.
TONI	I suddenly feel so, small.
JANE	I suddenly feel so /
TONI	I'm sorry.
JANE	I'm sorry.
TONI	And I hold her by the shoulders and ask her to stop. I'm sorry. I'm sorry. I pay her double and can't stop telling her I'm sorry. I'm sorry... I was just trying to... I wanted to be... and I look her in the face, and I promise I won't forget it. I won't forget.
JANE	I stare at the puddle next to me, expecting to see a reflection but I don't see anything. Just a never-ending nothingness.
TONI	I just wanted to be on the other side of it all. For once. I want to be the other side of it all. For. Once.

JANE   This isn't me.

TONI   But that means she had to be… and I'm sorry.
            I just…

JANE   Or maybe it is me.

TONI   I thought I knew what I wanted.

JANE   (*Together.*) Fuck.

TONI   (*Together.*) Fuck.

            And when she returns home she crawls into the
            safety of her clean bedsheets she listens to her
            children hurry down the hall. Her head hurts and
            her eyes wet with the relief of returning.

JANE   She arrives at his door and he is surprised to see
            her. She slips off her jacket to reveal her hangover
            and her hurt.

TONI   And he takes me in his arms.

JANE   And it's his skin on hers.

TONI   And I just wanted to be held.

JANE   And there is pressure in his palms.

TONI   I just want to be held.

JANE   And he unzips his fly. And he flips up her skirt /

TONI   And my body resists.

            And my body resists.

            Why can't he feel my body resisting?

            I just…

            I just want…

JANE   And she watches herself in the mirror opposite.
            Watching his body hand into hers.

TONI   I just wanted to…

JANE   And in between the blurring of the rules and her burning skin, shame washes over her. The shiny, sharp, serrated sensation of shame.

TONI   And I think about my father and what he would have thought. And I think about his kind eyes and his gentle joyful way. And how I wish he was here. And I think of my mother and what she would have thought. And I think about how I have her hands and her need to please and feed. And how I wish she was here. And I think of my father's father and my mother's mother and all their parents and partners and pain. I think about their pain. A long line of humans who have led to me being here. And her as he watches me get dressed, I think about how we have all been looked at but never really seen. And I just want someone to finally see me. All of me.

JANE   And she stares at herself in the mirror.

TONI   Before we take off /

JANE   A Swiss Army knife of a life.

TONI   Your captain asks /

JANE   Shiny and sharp.

TONI   Simply lift up the metal flap /

JANE   And the ground shakes.

TONI   And pull /

JANE   And as she picks up her underwear it turns to sand.

TONI   And pull apart /

JANE   The sand slips through her fingers.

TONI   And pull /

JANE   And there is a shudder below her /

TONI   And as she waits at the gates to collect her
          children. She watches the other mothers smile and
          make small talk about nothing at all and as she
          plays with the lipstick in her pocket it turns to lint.

JANE   Is this it? Is this really it?

TONI   And she reminds herself that she has everything
          she has ever wanted.

JANE   You know you should sell that flat you spend such
          little time in it.

TONI   Yeah, maybe.

JANE   They keep on putting me on flights with girls that
          need training. They all seem so young and none of
          them know how to drink. I miss you when you're
          not around.

TONI   I know.

JANE   You're always so… busy. Your life is so… cool.

TONI   What makes my life cool?

JANE   Because it's not mine.

TONI   It's not a competition.

JANE   Then why does it feel like one?

TONI   I don't know.

JANE   Are you okay?

TONI   I just…

JANE   Do you want a drink?

TONI   Jane?

          Silence.

          Make mine a large glass of /

JANE   LA and Leeds.

TONI   And Leon.

JANE   And Taipei.

TONI   And Glasgow.

JANE   And Granada and Madrid and Manila and
         Marrakech and /

TONI   Continents collide /

JANE   Countries and currencies cut into /

TONI   Earth becomes ocean, ocean becomes earth /

JANE   A populus of people pulses /

TONI   A lifetime of lives.

JANE   There is no end /

TONI   There is no defining moment /

JANE   There is no change when everything is changing
         all the /

TONI   Show me where it hurts.

JANE   Show me how it hurts.

TONI   Show me /

JANE   All of history heaves its way /

TONI   All of history and how terrible we treat each /

JANE   Have you seen the news?

TONI   Did they offer you it?

JANE   What?

TONI   The promotion?

JANE   Where did that come from?

TONI   Did they offer you it?

JANE   The promotion? No.

TONI   Do you know how hard I'd been trying for it?
         How many shit shifts I've done, bending over
         backwards… and they gave it to someone else.

JANE	Do you know who?
TONI	I'd been really gunning for that.
JANE	I'm sorry.
TONI	I really wanted that.
JANE	I know.
TONI	I'd been really… that was meant to be…
JANE	I know.
TONI	I am trying to be better. Get better. I am trying.
JANE	I know.
TONI	And it's all been ignored. All for nothing. Working myself to the… and none of it mattered.
JANE	I'm sure next time there is /
TONI	Do you remember when we really wanted this job?
JANE	I still want it.
TONI	But during training we wanted it.
JANE	I knew I wanted to be your friend.
TONI	But this job was our out. We both knew that. It was a way to get out of our lives. Out of our mothers' lives. It used to be good, didn't it? Really glamorous. Getting to go places I never dreamt of going. But it's changed. Hasn't it? The job used to be fun now it's fucking awful.
JANE	I still love it.
TONI	And the screaming and shouting starts to move closer.
JANE	You'll fall in love with it again. You're just tired.
TONI	And the ground begins to crack all around her.

JANE   You've just seen one too many hotel rooms this month. That can get to a girl. To be honest if I stay at home too much – that gets to me. I love my children but...

TONI   And neither of them blinks at it, even though both of them see it. Both of them know the ground is cracking and breaking below them, neither says a word.

JANE   Have you seen the news?

TONI   Yeah, terrible.

JANE   Just terrible.

TONI   That whole situation just seems so... terrible.

JANE   God, I know. I should donate some money.

TONI   And as she sits in a hotel room just east of anywhere, she turns on the television and there is nothing but fuzz, she flicks through a magazine and there is blank pages where print should be. And she isn't sure if it's her or the world which is disappearing. And she picks up her phone to call her children who always greet and meet her with smiles and kisses and she doesn't think she can handle their kindness. That their kindness might kill her because for a reason that remains undiscovered even to herself she doesn't feel deserving of it. And it all just /

JANE   It all just /

TONI   Have you watched /

JANE   Something is /

TONI   Have you seen what's happening?

JANE   Something is coming back.

        Show me where it hurts.

TONI   And all of history just /

JANE	Show me how it hurts.
TONI	Are you coming or going?
JANE	Just landed – Rio. Are you coming or going?
TONI	I'm just about to fly out – New York.
JANE	Me and my mother have been sitting in silence for thirty minutes during which time she smokes five cigarettes and drinks a double vodka. She begins to tell me another story about how life has wronged her.
TONI	And before I know it. I'm in the car, sitting in his driveway.
JANE	I feel a flame of jealousy for those who go misty-eyed when they talk about their mothers.
TONI	And before I know it. I'm at his front door. And I ring his bell.
JANE	And I sit staring at her.
TONI	And no one answers.
JANE	Trying to see something of me in there.
TONI	And I ring his bell.
JANE	And I keep looking
TONI	And I ring his bell.
JANE	And I keep looking
TONI	And I ring his bell.
JANE	And all I see is a lesson in how not to live.
TONI	I just wanted to be held.
JANE	On the drive home I tell the children that I love them, an inappropriate amount of times.
TONI	I just want to feel something inside of me.
JANE	And I tell them that no matter what – Mummy will always love you.

TONI	And I ring his bell.
JANE	And I promise to drink less.
TONI	And I ring his bell.
JANE	And I promise I won't be like what came before.
TONI	Please.
JANE	And when I get home I put the children to bed and I lock myself in the toilet.
TONI	Please.
JANE	And just at the edge of my eyeline, I notice a crack. Running its way through my nicely newly painted bathroom wall.
TONI	And I stand on his doorstep and I slip my hand down under my skirt and underwear.
JANE	I run my finger along it. I slip my finger into it.
TONI	And slip my fingers inside of myself.
JANE	And out comes plaster and paint.
JANE	(*Together.*) Fuck.
TONI	(*Together.*) Fuck.
TONI	And I twist my fingers inside myself.
JANE	I follow the crack.
TONI	And I reach inside myself.
JANE	I feel the gap.
TONI	And I reach inside myself.
JANE	I follow the crack.
TONI	And I reach inside myself.
JANE	I feel the gap.
TONI	And I reach inside myself.
JANE	Oh my god.

TONI   Fuck.

JANE   My house.

TONI   Please.

JANE   My home.

TONI   Someone.

JANE   You okay? You look a little /

TONI   I'm fine.

JANE   Good.

TONI   You?

JANE   Yeah.

          You know me.

          Always fine.

TONI   I better go – running late.

          See you.

JANE   Call me? We can catch up?

TONI   And she takes a can of the thickest brightest paint she can find.

JANE   And she sits with the television blaring of news of another shooting, south of somewhere. She sits on her sofa, picking off the lint.

TONI   And she takes a brush as thick as her fist.

JANE   And she picks at it with the tips of her fake nails.

TONI   And she crams the paint in the cracks.

JANE   Her face is puffy and painful from plucking and pruning.

TONI   And she crams the paint in the cracks.

JANE   And her legs are raw from the wounds of waxing.

TONI   And she crams the paint in the cracks.

JANE   And she feels clean.

TONI   And she crams the paint in the cracks.

JANE   And she picks at the lint.

TONI   And she crams the paint in the cracks.

JANE   And she picks at the lint until her fingernail snaps.
            And with blood dripping down her finger she feels
            the ground around her turn to sand. She goes to
            pick up the remote and it turns to dirt.

TONI   And splinters from the handle of the brush dig into
            her skin. Wood works its way into her palm and
            her pulse throbs in her fist. And she works past the
            pain. She works past the wound.

JANE   We'd like to remind you that smoking is not
            permitted onboard this /

TONI   And even when her husband holds her. In the most
            beautiful tender way.

JANE   Mobile phones must be placed in /

TONI   Even when her husband /

JANE   Always make sure your hand /

TONI   She can't stop feeling like /

JANE   Please place items in the overheard /

TONI   Like this is nothing and her pain feels pathetic and
            pointless. And all the newsprint and pictures and
            mirrors and even puddles have stopped reflecting
            her image. And she wonders what happens, what
            happens when you never see yourself anywhere.
            What part of you might also disappear.

JANE   And as blood falls out from between her legs,
            even her body is against her. Her stomach
            crunches with cramps and clots collect and she
            can't be bothered with it. A monthly reminder of
            something she'll never need. She doesn't even

want. And she is fine with it and wonders why no
one else is. And she works past /

TONI   She works past the wound.

JANE   She works past the world.

TONI   She works past the wound.

JANE   She works past /

TONI   The dirt.

JANE   The sand.

TONI   And soil.

JANE   And grit.

TONI   And shit. She works past the wound.

JANE   She works past the world.

TONI   She works past the wound.

JANE   She works past /

TONI   The dirt.

JANE   The sand.

TONI   And soil.

JANE   And grit.

TONI   And shit. The dirt.

JANE   The sand.

TONI   And soil.

JANE   And grit.

TONI   And shit. Dirt.

JANE   Sand.

TONI   Soil.

JANE   Grit.

TONI	Shit.
JANE	This hotel is fucking awful.
TONI	Have you drank that bottle already?

Silence.

Jane?

It's a little early to have /

JANE	Subsidence.
TONI	What?
JANE	Subsidence. My house is sinking. Literally sinking into the ground.

All that work. All that money.

TONI	Doesn't your insurance /
JANE	It was our savings, our retirement fund, our... it was everything and now...
TONI	Do you want another drink?
JANE	I think this might kill me.

I genuinely think this might kill me.

When the man told me. The man who came over to look at the cracks – my heart stopped.

It's the soil. Changes in the soil.

TONI   Look. Maybe it's not that bad. Maybe your insurance will cover it.

It can't be just your house affected. I'm sure if you talk to your neighbours, you'll find a way to work it out.

And it might not cost that much, plus it's not like John's family aren't short of a penny or /

JANE   Oh, fuck you.

TONI   Excuse me?

JANE   Fuck you.

TONI   You're drunk.

            Let's get you a glass of water. We've got a flight
            in /

JANE   When I walk /

TONI   When I walk into a room in my uniform.

JANE   There is a look that gets thrown my way.

TONI   When I walk into a room in my uniform.

JANE   And you're right – they offered me that
            promotion. The boys in charge said, we like her,
            we really like her, you seem like a reliable family
            woman. A good role model for modern women.
            Move her up to business class, they said. And you
            know what – I'm still considering it.

TONI   Good for you.

JANE   You find it impossible to be happy for me.

TONI   That's not true.

JANE   All these years and all you've done is make fun
            and dragged me down. You've made me feel so
            shit for having children. Do you know that? And
            why do you think that is?

TONI   I think you've had enough to drink. I think you've
            had more than enough to /

JANE   You're lonely. That's what it is, isn't it? No family.
            Barely a boyfriend. And I can just about justify
            you not liking my children because you don't have
            any of your own.

TONI   I don't want children.

JANE   Stop kidding yourself.

TONI   I don't want children.

JANE   For I am the image of /

TONI   A symbol of /

JANE   All high heels /

TONI   Navy and /

JANE   And I am /

TONI   And I am /

JANE   And I am /

TONI   And I am /

JANE   Oh, please.

You'd be a terrible mother, anyway. Because all you care about is fucking that guy. Not that you love him, because you wouldn't know love if it came and slapped you in the face. Because all you do is push people away, you push and you push and you push.

And the truth is – I don't know how to help you because you are beyond help. You used to be fun, now you're just fucked.

TONI   At least I don't live in a bubble of paint choices and Pinot Grigio.

JANE   I have worked damn hard my entire life for every last scrap of anything so don't you dare tell me what I do and don't deserve. You're jealous, you've always been jealous.

TONI   I'm not jealous of you.

JANE   Yeah, right.

TONI   Yeah, right. Not every woman is jealous of another. I work really hard at not being jealous. Even though everything wants me to be. Even though everything is designed for us to be jealous of each other, as if jealousy is the only emotion women have for one another – but it's not. Even though – everything – is designed to remind me of all the things I – supposedly – lack.

Because don't you hate the way we are meant to /

JANE   Do you know what I hate?

TONI   Your life.

Silence.

JANE   What did you…

Silence.

TONI   You hate your life.

And I can see why you would.

Silence.

I've heard you cry at night. Hotel walls can be very thin.

JANE   I said that wasn't me.

TONI   But it was.

Silence.

JANE   You know what makes this worse.

We chose each other. Me and you. We chose each other. What? Near twenty years ago. We chose each other.

And look how wrong we got it. Look how wrong I got it.

TONI   Fuck you.

JANE   Fuck you.

TONI   And Belfast and Budapest and Moscow and Melbourne and Mexico City and Cape Town and Amol and Amsterdam and /

JANE   Rocks and rubble rub up against me.

TONI	Continents collide /
JANE	Countries and currencies cut into /
TONI	Earth becomes ocean, ocean becomes earth /
JANE	A populus of people pulses /
TONI	A lifetime of lives.
JANE	There is no end /
TONI	There is no defining moment /
JANE	There is no change when everything is changing all the /
TONI	Show me where it hurts.
JANE	Show me how it hurts.
TONI	Show me /
JANE	It's just soil and soot and shit and stuff all crushed up against /
TONI	The expectation of existence.
JANE	All of history heaves its way /
TONI	All of history and how terrible we treat each /
JANE	Have you seen the news?
TONI	It's just awful.
JANE	And all of history just /
TONI	We soften parts of ourselves.
JANE	We erase parts of ourselves to become palatable.
TONI	Because I look around and I don't see anyone like me. Because I look around and I cannot find myself anywhere. I cannot place myself anywhere. And I have been all around the world, watched everything in every language and still... And what happens... What happens to me if I cannot see myself.

JANE   And she turns on the television, the radio, her phone, her computer all to top volume.

TONI   And she drives through the city, her hands on her steering wheel. Gripping on to it as if her life depends on it.

JANE   Voices and the sound of bombs and gunfire fill the room.

TONI   The end of some side road in the middle of nowhere in particular. She climbs out of her car and falls to her knees.

JANE   (*Together.*) And she screams.

TONI   (*Together.*) And she screams.

TONI   Until she thinks her throat might rip.

JANE   And then she turns off everything, all the lights, closes the curtains. And she lays down.

TONI   And she steps back into her car. She closes the door behind her and begins to cry.

JANE   And she opens a packet of sleeping pills. Anything for some silence and stillness. Anything.

TONI   And she wraps her arms around herself. Holding on to herself. And with that the ground begins to tremble.

JANE   And from below they both begin to hear this groan.

          This guttural groan.

TONI   The noise of something cracking and splitting and breaking away.

          The distant noise of tremors and change and growing and grasping and groaning.

JANE   Something trying to get out.

TONI   Something trying to find me.

JANE   And a hand bursts through the ground reaching up at me.

         And another hand and another hand.

         Grasping. Groping. Grasping. Groping.

TONI   Hands. Up from the ground. Hundreds of hands.

JANE   Peeling back the pavement.

TONI   Cracking the concrete.

JANE   All around.

TONI   Seas of hands and fingernails. Digging themselves out of the ground.

JANE   Digging themselves out of the earth. Hands with pink-painted nails. Hands with promise rings and tattooed knuckles. They are all women.

TONI   Raising themselves up.

JANE   The women are digging themselves up.

TONI   Clawing at the dirt. They are climbing back, to claim back. Hands through the dirt. Hundreds of hands, clawing through the dirt.

         The women are climbing back, to claim back. They are climbing back from the beyond.

JANE   Every shape and shade and size.

TONI   Every shape and shade and size.

JANE   The women pull themselves up and out the ground. Hundreds of women. And she stands before them and they stand looking at her.

TONI   Covered in dirt and sand and soil and sick and shit and blood and /

JANE   Covered in anger and exhaustion and anticipation /

TONI   And one of them reaches out her hands. And she takes me in her arms.

I just want to be held.

I just want… and she holds me.

And the pain and shame and hate and hurt and…
it drains away. In her arms. The pain drains away.

Silence.

JANE   And she knows there are too many. Too many
images. Too many meanings. But life is not
singular. Life is many and messy. At least her life
is – many messy things.

TONI   And she knows that we soften the edges and
become singular. We soften the edges and become
singular. And we have no idea we're doing it.

JANE   Because there is no end.

TONI   There is no defining moment.

Phone call.

JANE   Toni.

It's me.

I don't know where I am, I drove and drove and
drove until…

But it's beautiful here. It's really… calm.

And I just… I just wish you were here.

That's what people say isn't it?

I wish you were here, I wish you were here, I wish
you were here, I wish you were here, I wish you
were…

I think this might kill me.

I genuinely think this might kill me and I don't
even know what this is and…

Call me.

Please.

	Before we take off, your captain asks that you familiarise yourself with our safety procedures and equipment.
TONI	Whenever the sign is on, fasten your seatbelt securely. Insert the metal tag into the buckle and tighten by pulling on the loose end.
JANE	To undo the belt, simply lift up the metal flap on the buckle and pull apart.
TONI	And pull apart.
JANE	And pull apart.
TONI	And pull apart.
JANE	And pull /
TONI	Hello.
JANE	Hello.
TONI	Hello.
JANE	Hello.
	Silence.
TONI	I was surprised to see you on the flight. I'd heard you'd taken some time off.
JANE	I wanted to be with the kids.
	I called you. I was worried something had…
TONI	Yeah. I just… I didn't have any words… for you.
JANE	I'm sorry for…
TONI	Me too.
	Silence.
JANE	I was really angry.
TONI	I know.
JANE	And I just want you to be happy. Happy with that guy /

TONI   He did things. Terrible things.

            I thought I was okay with…

            I thought I was okay.

            But I'm not.

JANE   What did he /

TONI   Terrible things.

            I'm trying to stop seeing him. I'm trying really
            hard to stop.

JANE   Good.

TONI   It's been hard.

JANE   I know.

TONI   No. You don't.

            Silence.

JANE   You were wrong when you said I hated my life.
            I don't hate my life. I love my husband and my
            children so fiercely that… they are my life. They
            are the life I always wanted.

            But…

            But. I think I might hate myself.

            Which is a strange and very specific thing to learn
            about yourself. And it's a true clear icy hate.

            For years I have felt like I wasn't worth the air
            I breathed. I held my breath for decades.

            And then I realised, when I am away, away from
            myself. I could exhale. Because I was someone
            new or rather – I could be all the bits I like about
            myself.

            I was no one and someone.

            That's the beauty of being anonymous it makes life
            seem ginormous. I wanted life to feel big again.

And that is why I love you so much.

You were an escape. And I'm sorry.

Because you are so much more than that. You are so much more than that to me.

Silence.

TONI   It's hard. Isn't it? To take care of yourself. In a world that isn't designed for you.

Silence.

JANE   I love you.

TONI   And I love you.

Silence.

Jane?

JANE   Yeah?

TONI   Something is happening... I've been... I've felt things.

JANE   I have too.

Silence.

TONI   And what does it mean?

JANE   I don't know.

Silence.

TONI   Do you feel like we are being left behind?

JANE   I don't know.

Silence.

TONI   When I walk into a room, in my uniform.

JANE   There is a look that gets thrown my way.

TONI   When I walk into a room, in my uniform.

JANE   It's as if for a second...

Silence.

TONI   The two of us must be a sight.

Two fully dressed air hostesses standing in the desert, surrounded by nothing but cactuses and climate change. All navy-blue and nylons. It's hard to walk on sand in heels. Should have taken them off, should have done a lot of things.

But right now, out of her handbag she produces a miniature of whisky. I've never liked whisky – until now. Now standing in this desert in the back-end of nowhere, sweating through my shirt, I like whisky. I want to be the type of woman who likes whisky and so I will be.

The cap snaps.

Down in one.

She passes me another.

The cap snaps. Down in one.

I'm already a bottle deep into drunkenness and can sense I'll have the Chardonnay shits in the morning.

JANE   And in time my feet will blister, my nail polish will chip, and I'll cry and call my husband across eight time zones to tell him I love him.

And she reaches out and I slip her hand into mine.

We might be two grown women, but our teenage selves are twinkling through our wrinkles.

Her palm pulses in mine. I squeeze it. I squeeze it as tight as I can. And by doing that I am telling her – *I'm so sorry*. In total silence I tell her – *I am so sorry for what the world has done to us*.

And I don't need to look at her to know she is crying. Her hand is shaking in mine. The vibration of a silent, deep, weep. The kind of cry that has been creeping in shadows for centuries.

Because standing here in the sand – we both know
this particular ache, this particular anger is…
ancient.

TONI   Don't you think it's beautiful?

JANE   It's certainly something.

             You've always liked places like this. You've
             always enjoyed…

TONI   What?

JANE   Discomfort.

TONI   Is that what you'd call it?

JANE   Yeah.

TONI   Maybe I'd just gotten used to the discomfort.

             I'd gotten used to feeling raw and sore and being
             hard and hidden and… I don't want to hide
             any more.

             I'm so tired of hiding parts of me.

             I'm done with hiding.

JANE   But what if they /

TONI   I don't care.

             Silence.

             I can't care.

JANE   And the women wonder who else is still below.
             They wonder who else is being left behind.

TONI   And with that thought the women begin to slip
             into the sand. They'd been warned about this. The
             wind is picking up and the sand is collecting at
             their feet.

JANE   There is a storm heading their way and the sand
             begins to gather at their feet. The sand begins to
             build around them. But neither of them flinch.
             Neither of them mind.

TONI   Because they are prepared. Because they have each other. Because something is starting to make sense. Something that exists beyond any words either of them know.

JANE   She turns to her friend and nods. And with that she dives her hands into the ground.

TONI   And with that she dives her hands into the ground.

JANE   (*Together.*) And she lets out a roar from the bottom of her stomach.

TONI   (*Together.*) And she lets out a roar from the bottom of her stomach.

JANE   And the two women begin to dig.

TONI   They dig to free themselves.

JANE   They dig to free so much more than themselves.

TONI   They continue to dig and dig.

JANE   And they toil in the dirt and dust of it.

TONI   They toil in the blood and burn of it.

JANE   They dig and they dig and dig.

TONI   And they won't ever stop.

JANE   The women dig.

TONI   They keep digging.

JANE   They dig forever.

A Nick Hern Book

Enough first published as a paperback original in Great Britain in 2019 by Nick Hern Books Limited, The Glasshouse, 49a Goldhawk Road, London W12 8QP, in association with the Traverse Theatre, Edinburgh

Designed and typeset by Nick Hern Books, London
Printed in the UK by Mimeo Ltd, Huntingdon, Cambridgeshire PE29 6XX

A CIP catalogue record for this book is available from the British Library

ISBN 978 1 84842 845 4

Woodland
CARBON
www.woodlandcarbon.co.uk
NICK HERN BOOKS
Printed on Carbon Captured paper